FUNNEL-WEB SPIDER

by Rachel Rose

Minneapolis, Minnesota

Credits
Cover and title page, © Ken Griffiths/iStock; 4–5, © Sahara Frost/Adobe Stock; 7, © Ken Griffiths/Adobe Stock; 8–9, © Ken Griffiths/Getty Images; 11, © Akima Futura/Alamy; 12–13, © Ken Griffiths/Shutterstock; 13, © Ken Griffiths/Adobe Stock; 14, © soleg/iStock; 14–15, © Patti Murray/Animals Animals; 16–17, © Ken Griffiths/Adobe Stock; 18–19, © Ken Griffiths/iStock; 20–21, © Photography by Mangiwau/Getty Images; 22, © Ken Griffiths/Shutterstock.

Bearport Publishing Company Product Development Team
President: Jen Jenson; Director of Product Development: Spencer Brinker; Managing Editor: Allison Juda; Associate Editor: Naomi Reich; Associate Editor: Tiana Tran; Art Director: Colin O'Dea; Designer: Elena Klinkner; Designer: Kayla Eggert; Product Development Assistant: Owen Hamlin

STATEMENT ON USAGE OF GENERATIVE ARTIFICIAL INTELLIGENCE
Bearport Publishing remains committed to publishing high-quality nonfiction books. Therefore, we restrict the use of generative AI to ensure accuracy of all text and visual components pertaining to a book's subject. See BearportPublishing.com for details.

Library of Congress Cataloging-in-Publication Data

Names: Rose, Rachel, 1968- author.
Title: Funnel-web spider / by Rachel Rose.
Description: Minneapolis : Bearport Publishing Company, [2024] | Series: Danger down under | Includes bibliographical references and index.
Identifiers: LCCN 2023030966 (print) | LCCN 2023030967 (ebook) | ISBN 9798889164968 (library binding) | ISBN 9798889165033 (paperback) | ISBN 9798889165095 (ebook)
Subjects: LCSH: Agelenidae--Juvenile literature.
Classification: LCC QL458.42.A3 R67 2024 (print) | LCC QL458.42.A3 (ebook) | DDC 595.4/4--dc23/eng/20230710
LC record available at https://lccn.loc.gov/2023030966
LC ebook record available at https://lccn.loc.gov/2023030967

Copyright ©2024 Bearport Publishing Company. All rights reserved. No part of this publication may be reproduced in whole or in part, stored in any retrieval system, or transmitted in any form or by any means, electronic, mechanical, photocopying, recording, or otherwise, without written permission from the publisher.

For more information, write to Bearport Publishing, 5357 Penn Avenue South, Minneapolis, MN 55419.

CONTENTS

Got Ya! 4
Burrow Homes 6
As Big as an Egg 8
Silken Threads 10
Toxic Venom 12
On the Menu 14
Humans Beware 16
Wanderers 18
Danger Cycle 20

More about Funnel-Web Spiders 22
Glossary 23
Index 24
Read More 24
Learn More Online 24
About the Author 24

GOT YA!

There's danger Down Under!

A hungry creature waits just out of sight in its **burrow**. When it senses **prey** crawling across its web, the funnel-web spider jumps into action. It quickly traps its victim and takes a deadly bite. Soon, dinner is served for this big, Australian spider.

> **!** These spiders get their name from the shape of their webs.

BURROW HOMES

There are about 40 different kinds of funnel-web spiders. Many are found in forests and cities along Australia's east coast and on the Australian island of Tasmania. These spiders make their burrow homes in spaces that are cool and moist, such as under rocks, in tree trunks, or even under houses!

> **!** The Sydney funnel-web spider is one of the world's deadliest spiders. As the name suggests, it's found near the city of Sydney, Australia.

A Sydney funnel-web spider

AS BIG AS AN EGG

As far as spiders go, funnel-webs are big. Their bodies can grow up to 2 inches (5 cm) long—about the size of a chicken's egg! These spiders are usually brown or black, and they have two main body parts. A glossy, hard **thorax** is in the front, and a softer, hairy **abdomen** is behind. Like all spiders, funnel-webs have eight legs and two **fangs**.

The funnel-web spider has eight eyes that are close together.

SILKEN THR[EADS]

The funnel-web spider spins it[s] thread that comes out of its ab[domen] a long tunnel-shaped weaving with [an] opening at one end.

The spider also spins silk trip lines that spr[ead] away from the entrance of its burrow. Then, the funnel-web spider hides inside and waits. The trip lines will let the spider know when prey is nearby.

!

Some funnel-web burrows have two entrances. These web homes are shaped like a Y.

A funnel-web spider's burrow entrance

TOXIC VENOM

When something walks across one of the trip lines, the spider feels the movement and darts out of the burrow. Once it has captured its next meal, the spider bites with its large, sharp fangs. The fangs inject dangerous **venom** that can kill some prey within minutes. Then, the funnel-web spider drags its meal back into the burrrow and feasts.

! A funnel-web spider's fangs are so sharp and strong that they can bite through some shoes.

ON THE MENU

Funnel-web spiders eat mostly **insects**, such as beetles and cockroaches. They also feed on other small animals, such as lizards and frogs. Even though their venom is very harmful, not all animals are affected by it. Birds, cats, and dogs can survive the spider's bite.

Many chickens gobble up funnel-web spiders as a tasty snack.

HUMANS BEWARE

The funnel-web's venom is dangerous to humans. A bite is painful, and the venom can make a person throw up and have trouble breathing. Some people have even died from funnel-web spider bites. Luckily, scientists have created an **antivenom** to help people who have been bitten.

Antivenom is medicine for a venomous bite. A person bitten by a funnel-web may die unless they get antivenom quickly.

WANDERERS

Humans are most likely to come across funnel-web spiders during **mating** season. This is the time when **male** spiders wander far from their burrows in search of **females**.

Once the spiders have mated, the females lay up to 200 eggs in sacs woven from silk. The eggs will stay there for about a month.

!

Sometimes, a male and female spider will **spar**, or fight with each other before they mate.

A funnel-web spider ready to spar

DANGER CYCLE

After the baby spiders hatch, they stay with their mothers for several months. Then, they leave to make their own burrows. When they are about four years old, the funnel-web spiders are ready to mate and start the cycle again. Watch out for this danger Down Under!

!

Male spiders live just past the age of 4, while females can live for up to 20 years!

MORE ABOUT FUNNEL-WEB SPIDERS

⚠ The fangs of funnel-web spiders are bigger than the fangs of some small snakes!

⚠ Most funnel-web spiders live in burrows near the ground, but there are a few kinds that live in trees.

⚠ These spiders can't swim, but they can trap a small bubble of air in the hairs of their abdomens, which helps them float.

⚠ Funnel-webs use the trapped air to breathe underwater, too. The spiders have been known to survive for up to 30 hours without coming up for air.

⚠ The male funnel-web spider's venom is about six times more toxic than the female's.

⚠ When these spiders need to move around, they usually do it at night to stay out of the hot Australian sun.

GLOSSARY

abdomen the back part of a spider's body

antivenom a medicine that blocks the effects of venom

burrow a hole or tunnel used by a spider as its home

fangs sharp parts of a spider's mouth used to bite and inject venom

females spiders that can lay eggs

insects small animals with bodies that have three parts and six legs

male a spider that cannot lay eggs

mating coming together to have young

prey an animal that is hunted and eaten by another animal

spar to strike or attack

thorax the front part of a spider's body that includes its head

venom poison from a spider that is injected through fangs

Index

abdomen 8–10, 22
burrow 4, 6, 10–12, 18, 20, 22
female 18, 20, 22
insect 14
male 18, 20, 22
mating 18, 20
prey 4, 10, 12
Sydney funnel-web spider 7
Tasmania 6
thorax 8–9
trip lines 10, 12
venom 12, 14, 16, 22

Read More

Hofer, Charles. *Tiny but Deadly Critters (Killer Nature).* North Mankato, MN: Capstone Press, 2022.

Santos, Tracie. *Spiders and Other Arthropods (Dangerous . . . or Not?).* Vero Beach, FL: Rourke Educational Media, 2021.

Learn More Online

1. Go to **www.factsurfer.com** or scan the QR code below.
2. Enter "**Funnel-Web Spider**" into the search box.
3. Click on the cover of this book to see a list of websites.

About the Author

Rachel Rose writes books for kids and teaches yoga. Her favorite animal of all is her dog, Sandy.